Magical Things

I am Epic

A.T. YOUNG

Copyright

Title book: Magical Things
Sub Title: I am Epic
Author: A.T. Young
Illustration: A.T. Young
Published:Thinking Spirit Press

© 2025 A.T. Young
www.thinkingspirit.com
First edition 2025

For more information, please contact:

author@thinkingspirit.com

Thank you for our support

Dedicated to my best friend, Rebecca

I shine with light from deep inside,

my outer glow is filled with pride.

With sparkling eyes and grounded grace,

I walk with power in every place.

My body's sacred, strong and free,

just as the Universe made me!

I look divine, just as I'm meant to be!

My mind creates what comes my way,

through thoughts I build a brighter day.

With words I speak, with dreams I dare,

I manifest with love and care.

Each idea's a guiding star

and what I think is who we are!

My thoughts are seeds of magic and light!

I think of joy and skies so blue,

of mountains climbed and wishes true.

Of kindness growing all around,

of love and laughter that's abound.

My thoughts are strong and clear and bold,

they shape my life in dreams of gold!

I think with purpose, power and peace!

Some might not see the light I hold,

or know the stories yet untold.

But I stand tall and rise above,

I know I'm worthy, I know I'm love.

Their thoughts can't change my shining core,

I'm more myself than ever before!

What matters most is what I believe!

When life feels hard or takes a turn,

I pause, reflect and gently learn.

I breathe in peace and let fear go,

my inner strength begins to grow.

The answers come when I am still,

I move with trust and grounded will!

I release and rise with calm and grace!

I turn to light, I ask for signs,

the Universe sends loving lines.

I journal, speak and move with flow,

I water seeds I want to grow.

I take each step with open heart,

from fear to faith, I play my part!

I turn my struggles into stars!

I smile at sunbeams on my face,

I dance with joy and soft embrace.

I love when silence brings me peace,

or when my worries find release.

Happiness comes from deep inside,

it's not a place, it's how I ride!

Joy is my natural state of being!

One day at a time, I walk my way,

through ups and downs, come what may.

I trust my path, I trust the flow,

each twist and turn helps me to grow.

No storm can dim my shining soul,

I move ahead, complete and whole!

I am guided. I am grounded. I am growing!

I've learned that thoughts are mighty things,

that trust and truth give me my wings.

That love is strong and fear is weak

and every soul is born unique.

Each lesson shapes the path I take,

each dream I plant, each choice I make!

I am always learning with love and light!

I'll speak kind words and take deep rest,

I'll try each day to do my best.

I'll set clear goals and honour me,

I'll manifest what's meant to be.

I'll listen close, I'll give and grow

and trust in all I deeply know!

I hold the power to change my life!

I'll shine my light, so others see,

the strength and joy inside of me.

I'll speak with love, I'll share with care

and lift the hearts that need repair.

I'll walk beside them through the rain

and help them rise through all their pain!

My light helps others find their way!

Thank you for reading this book. Please use the blank pages for your paperback book notes

www.ingramcontent.com/pod-product-compliance
Lightning Source LLC
Chambersburg PA
CBHW041558040426
42447CB00002B/214